MALAYSIA

Jane Hinchey

REDBACK
publishing

First Published 2021 by
Redback Publishing
PO Box 357 Frenchs Forest NSW 2086
Australia

www.redbackpublishing.com
orders@redbackpublishing.com

ISBN 978-1-922322-08-1

Author: Jane Hinchey
Editor: Marlene Vaughan
Design: Redback Publishing

Original illustrations © Redback Publishing 2021
Originated by Redback Publishing
Printed and bound in China

Acknowledgements
Abbreviations: l—left, r—right, b—bottom, t—top, c—centre, m—middle
We would like to thank the following for permission to reproduce
photographs: (Images © shutterstock) P6t Boddhisattva Maitreya by Gunawan Kartapran via
Wikipedia. p17bl Aznan

Every effort has been made to contact copyright holders of any material
reproduced in this book. Any omissions will be rectified in subsequent
printings if notice is given to the publisher.

Disclaimer
All the internet addresses (URLs) given in this book were valid at the time of going to press.
However, due to the dynamic nature of the internet, some addresses may have changed, or
sites may have changed or ceased to exist since publication. While the author and publisher
regret any inconvenience this may cause readers, no responsibility for any such changes can
be accepted by either the author or the publisher.

A catalogue record for this
book is available from the
National Library of Australia

MIX
Paper from
responsible sources
FSC® C020056

CONTENTS

MAP OF MALAYSIA

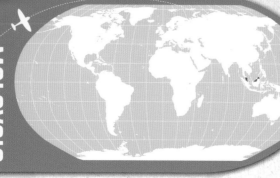

MALAYSIA

Bodgaya Mabul Island

BORNEO

THAILAND

PENANG

Kuala Terengganu

MEDAN

NORTH SUMATRA

Kuala Lumpur

PUTRAJAYA

MELAKA

SINGAPORE

Johor

WEST SUMATRA

Malaysia

MOUNT KINABALU

Sabah

Sarawak

NORTH KALIMANTAN

Kuching

CENTRAL KALIMANTAN

EAST KALIMANTAN

Eagle Square

LANGKAWI

Malacca City

MELAKA

Tea plantation

CAMERON HIGHLANDS

FUN FACTS

- Borneo is the third largest island in the world, after Greenland and New Guinea.

- The national animal of Malaysia is the endangered Malayan tiger. In 2016, it was estimated that only 3,890 of these tigers were left.

- The world's longest king cobra was caught in Malaysia, measuring 5.54 metres.

SNAPSHOT

COUNTRY

Malaysia

CAPITAL

Kuala Lumpur

OFFICIAL LANGUAGE

Bahasa Malaysia

AREA

329,758 square kilometres

POPULATION

32,772,100 (June 2019)

RELIGIONS Sunni Islam (official), Buddhist, Hindu, Christian

CURRENCY	€Ringgit
GOVERNMENT	Kuala Lumpur is the legislative capital, Putrajaya is the administrative capital

HIGHEST POINT Mount Kinabalu at 4,094 metres

City Skyline

KUALA LUMPUR

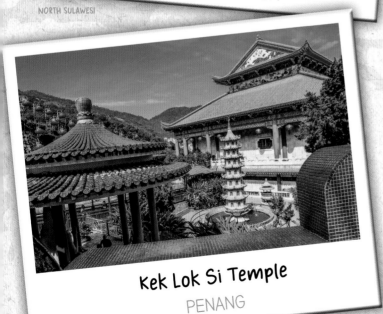

Kek Lok Si Temple

PENANG

MANILA

NORTH SULAWESI

PAPUA NEW GUINEA

Malaysia is a fascinating country located north of the equator in Southeast Asia. It was home to empires such as the Srivijaya, the Majapahit and the Melaka Sultanate, before being colonised by the Portuguese, Dutch and British. Today it is a vibrant, modern nation. It is a federal constitutional monarchy.

The world's tallest statue of Murugan
BATU CAVES

Malaysia has a population of over 31 million people, from diverse ethnic, religious and language groups.

Malaysia has the fourth largest economy in Southeast Asia, and is the second biggest producer in the world of palm oil. Other industries include rubber, light manufacturing industry, logging, petroleum production and refining.

Latex extracted from rubber tree

Malaysia is made up of two main landmasses, Peninsular Malaysia and Malaysian Borneo, separated by the South China Sea.

MALAYSIA

Malaysia has a population of over 31 million people. Over 75 per cent of them live in cities and urban areas. Malaysia's biggest cities are Kuala Lumpur and Klang. About 85 per cent of the population live on Peninsular Malaysia, while 15 per cent live in Sabah and Sarawak on Malaysian Borneo.

Malaysian fruit festival
KLANG

Malaysia is an ethnically diverse country, with Malays, Chinese, Indians and numerous indigenous peoples. Each group has its own religion, traditions and language, adding to the diversity of Malaysia.

Malay

In Malaysia, the term 'Malay' refers to a person who practises Islam and Malay traditions, speaks the Malay language and whose ancestors are Malays. Along with other aboriginal minorities, Malays are considered to be bumiputras, which means 'indigenous people'.

Chinese

Malaysian Chinese are the second largest ethnic group and have a long history in the area through maritime trade. Around 25 per cent of the overall population is Chinese.

Portuguese

There is a small community of descendants of the Portuguese in Malacca.

Indian

Most Indians are descended from Tamil-speaking labourers brought to Malaysia to work on rubber plantations during British colonial times. There are also small communities of Sikhs, Punjabis, Telugus and Sri Lankans.

Orang Asli

Orang Asli is a term that means original people, or aboriginal people.

Sarawak is home to 29 ethnic groups, the largest of which is the Iban, who are longhouse dwellers and rice planters.

Mount Kinabalu

Sarawak

Kuching

DAILY LIFE

Malaysians enjoy one of the highest standards of living in the region. Malays often live in apartment blocks and bungalows. Two-storey townhouses may be shared by two families with one family on each floor. As the official religion is Sunni Islam, Malaysians dress modestly.

Family is the focus of daily life and it's common to live with two or more generations.

Islamic Dress Code

Public servants are required to wear headscarves but are banned from wearing the burqa or the niqab. Most Muslim women wear headscarves, known as 'tudung', but it is not mandatory.

Health

The quality of healthcare in Malaysia is high, although cities tend to have better healthcare than rural areas. A government-run healthcare system operates side by side with private healthcare. Malaysia requires doctors to perform a mandatory three years in the public system to ensure a high standard of care in hospitals.

EDUCATION

Education is free in Malaysia and instruction takes place in Bahasa Malaysia, Chinese or Tamil. Almost all children attend primary school, starting at age six. After six years in primary school, children move into lower secondary. Although secondary years are not compulsory, 82 per cent of Malaysian children attend.

Malaysia has many universities, teacher training colleges and technical colleges, and a growing number of students study at these and at universities abroad.

Fast Fact

The world's first female to fly a MiG fighter plane was Patricia Yapp from Sabah.

FOOD

Malaysian cuisine incorporates an array of influences from all over Asia, along with local ingredients such as fresh vegetables and tropical fruits, seafood and spices.

Chilli is an important ingredient, as are shrimp paste, coconut and soy sauce. Common herbs are lemon grass, turmeric and the pandan leaf. Staples are rice, tofu, fish, pork and chicken.

Nasi lemak is a fragrant rice dish, often referred to as the national dish of Malaysia. It can be eaten at any time of the day, and hawker stalls selling nasi lemak are common.

SIX POPULAR MALAYSIAN DISHES ARE:

Nasi goreng
fried rice with meat
or prawns, eggs and
vegetables

Mee goreng
noodles with cabbage,
garlic, shallots and
chicken, prawns or pork

Rojak
fruit and
vegetable salad

Curry laksa
spicy curried
noodle soup

Fish head curry
the name describes this dish!

Roti canai
Indian flatbread

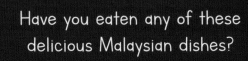

Have you eaten any of these
delicious Malaysian dishes?

LANGUAGE

There are 134 languages spoken in Malaysia and 112 of these are indigenous. The official language of Malaysia is Bahasa Malaysia, which is also called Malay. English is widely spoken and used in business.

Other languages spoken in Malaysia include: Mandarin, Cantonese, Kadazan, Gujarati, Telugu, Thai, Iban, Bengali, Kristang, Malayalam, Punjabi, Tamil, Sindhi, Foochow, Hokkien, Hakka, Teochew, Hainanese, Murut, Bajau, Dusun and Senoi.

Speak Bahasa Malaysia

Good Night
Selamat malam

Thank You
Terima kasih

Good Morning
Selamat pagi

Please
Tolong

I Don't Understand
Saya tidak faham

Good Afternoon
Selamat tengahari

HOW ARE YOU?
Apa khabar?

I'm fine
Khabar baik

AMAZING ARCHITECTURE

From modern city skylines
to traditional homes,
Malaysia's architecture
is as diverse as its people.

What is Colonialism?

When one country takes control or
imposes governance over another
country, territory or population.
The controlling country establishes
settlements or colonies.

Colonial Architecture

Portuguese, Dutch and English colonialists
brought their own architectural styles to
Malaysia, where they were modified according
to the tropical climate and combined with
other Asian influences. Areas of Kuala
Lumpur, Malacca, Penang (George Town) and the Cameron Highlands have strong colonial
influences, but it's not uncommon to see beautiful colonial buildings all over Malaysia.
Both George Town in Penang and Malacca now have World Heritage status as Historic
Towns. The unique shop houses of Malacca blend British, French and Chinese styles and
are known as Peranakan or Baba-Nyonya architecture.

Chinese Influence

Chinese dominance of commerce has
resulted in most towns and cities having
retail areas with Chinese shopfronts.

Petronas Towers

Petronas Towers, also known as the 'Petronas Twin Towers', is Kuala Lumpur's most famous landmark. From 1998 to 2004, the building was the tallest in the world. Today, it remains the tallest twin building in the world. The complex includes apartments, offices, one of Malaysia's largest shopping malls, an aquarium and science centre, an art gallery and a philharmonic theatre. There are 88 floors, with 40 lifts in each tower. The towers are joined by a skybridge on the 41st and 42nd floors. The view from the skybridge is a major tourist attraction.

Islamic Influence

Government administrative buildings in urban areas usually have Malay and Islamic architectural influences.

Dayak Longhouses

Borneo is home to over 200 ethnic groups, known as 'Dayaks'. Many Dayak groups, such as the Iban, live in communal dwellings that centre on one longhouse.

The construction of these buildings is a community affair. Each family has their own small living quarters, which adjoin a main communal longhouse. The entire building is raised from the forest floor on stilts.

The roof may be made from tiles, clay or palm branches

The roof flares upwards at each end to resemble ox horns. This style is called 'Minangkabau'

The walls are made from wood, bamboo or can be thatched

Under the eaves is an elaborate, wooden grillwork

Building a kampung house can take years. As the budget of the family grows, so does their home.

Kampung

Traditional Malay houses are found in villages called 'kampungs' or 'kampongs'. The houses are designed to meet the needs of living in a topical climate.

17

Malaysia can be divided into two parts: Peninsular Malaysia, also known as West Malaysia, and East Malaysia, which consists of two states in Borneo.

Malaysia's highest point is Mt. Kinabalu, at 4,100 metres; its lowest point is the South China Sea. The country is rich with geographical wonders—from islands and caves to mountain ranges and rainforests.

Sky bridge atop the rainforest
LANGKAWI ISLAND, WEST MALAYSIA

West Malaysia

West Malaysia borders Thailand to the north and is joined by a causeway to Singapore in the south, just across the Johor Strait. Four major mountain ranges dominate West Malaysia. Bordering these are the coastal lowlands, with mangrove swamps and flat fringes. This coastal region supports most of Malaysia's urban development and population.

Cave entrance
MULU NATIONAL PARK, BORNEO

East Malaysia

The flora and fauna-rich rainforests of East Malaysia are on Borneo and are shared with Indonesia and Brunei. This area boasts significant cave systems and one of the oldest rainforests in the world.

Climate

Malaysia lies just above the equator and enjoys a tropical climate all year round, rarely dropping below 25° Celsius, even in the cooler months. The rainy season is from December to March; the dry season is from June to September. In the highlands and mountains, temperatures can be cooler at night.

Fast Fact

Malaysia is one of the world's largest producers and exporters of palm oil

Orangutan

The red-haired orangutans of Borneo live in rainforests.

RELIGION AND FESTIVALS

Malaysia's constitution guarantees freedom of religion and the country is home to people of all faiths living in relative peace and harmony. Malaysia's official religion is Islam, practised by 61 per cent of Malaysians. All Malays are Muslim.

Other religions in Malaysia include Buddhism, Christianity, Hinduism, Taoism, Sikhism and Confucianism. In Borneo, major religions are Christianity, Islam and Buddhism/Taoism. Borneo's indigenous people still follow traditional beliefs, including animism and ancestor worship.

Islam

Indian traders brought Islam to Malaysia in the 12th century. There are many beautiful mosques in Malaysia including the National Mosque in Kuala Lumpur, which holds 16,000 people.

Major Muslim holidays and festivals include Hari Raya Puasa, which is a festival marking the end of Ramadan, and Awal Muharram, which is the Islamic New Year.

National Mosque of Malaysia
KUALA LUMPUR

Buddhism

Buddhism is the second largest religion in Malaysia. Most Chinese Malaysians practise Buddhism.

Major Buddhist holidays and festivals include Chinese New Year and the Dragon Boat Festival.

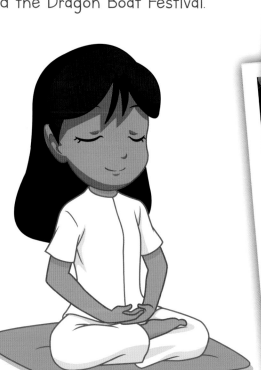

International Dragon Boat Festival
PUTRAJAYA MALAYSIA

Hinduism

While smaller than the other two main religions, there is still a prominent population of Hindus in Malaysia.

Major Hindu holidays and festivals include Deepavali or Diwali, "the Festival of Light". Pilgrims also converge on Batu Caves to celebrate Thaipusam.

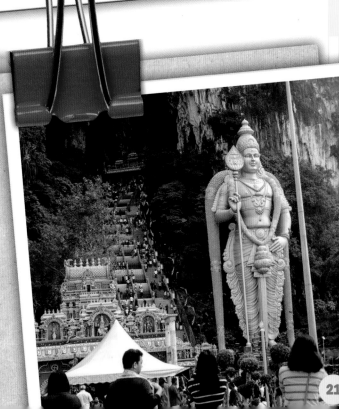

TRANSPORT

Public transport in Malaysia started to develop during British colonial rule. The country now has high-quality roads, railways and public transport services.

Car, Bike, and Bus

Car ownership in Malaysia is the third highest in the world, with 93 per cent of households owning a car. There is an extensive road network, including the North-South Expressway, which extends 800 kilometres from the Thailand to Singapore borders.

Malaysia's coach and minibus network is comprehensive, with express services between all major cities and most towns. Roads get very congested, so many people ride motorbikes and scooters.

An unusual mode of transport found in Malacca is the tuk tuk

Rail

Malaysian trains are inexpensive, efficient and modern, with extensive networks in the capital and for long distance travel.

The KTM ETS is an inter-city rail service, with the fastest train in Malaysia

Boat

Malaysia has a rich maritime history. With its 7,200 kilometres of waterways, it is strategically located on the Straits of Malacca and South China Sea international shipping routes. Ferries travel to Malaysian islands such as Penang, Langkawi, the Perhentians, Tioman and Pangkor..

TOURISM

Malaysia is home to many interesting and important historical sites. International tourism is a major contributor to Malaysia's economy.

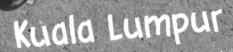

Kuala Lumpur

Kuala Lumpur is Malaysia's capital and the most populous city in the country Kuala Lumpur has become a popular tourist destination, and is renowned for its diversity, excellent cuisine and cheap shopping. The city boasts elegant colonial architecture and gleaming skyscrapers, the most recognisable being Petronas Towers.

Batu Caves

Just out of Kuala Lumpur are Batu Caves. These limestone caves are approximately 400 million years old and are the site for the most popular Hindu temple outside India. Pilgrims flock to the caves annually, to celebrate the Thaipusam Festival.

Statue of Hanuman, a Hindu god
RAMAYANA CAVE, BATU CAVES

Penang

Penang is a north-western state that is regarded as the food capital of Malaysia. Its culture is a vibrant blend of east and west. Penang's main city, George Town, is a UNESCO World Heritage area and one of Malaysia's most popular tourist destinations.

Island Hopping

Apart from Penang, Malaysia has hundreds of beautiful islands. Malaysians refer to their islands as 'Pulau'.

Can you find these Malaysian islands on a map?

- Langkawi
- Pulau Langkor
- Pulau Mabul
- Perhentian Islands
- Pulau Tioman

Parameswara, the Hindu prince

Malacca

Malacca, also spelt 'Melaka', is the name for both the state and the city and is a popular tourist destination. It has a rich maritime history, starting as a fishing village and later becoming the base for Parameswara, a Hindu prince from Sumatra. Under his rule, Malacca became a favoured shipping port on the spice route. The Portuguese took control of Malacca in 1511, and today the city retains a colonial influence in its architecture, which received World Heritage Listing in 2008.

Gunung Mulu national park

Kinabalu national park

World Heritage Sites

There are a total of four World Heritage Sites in Malaysia. Two are cultural and two are natural.

CULTURAL

CULTURAL

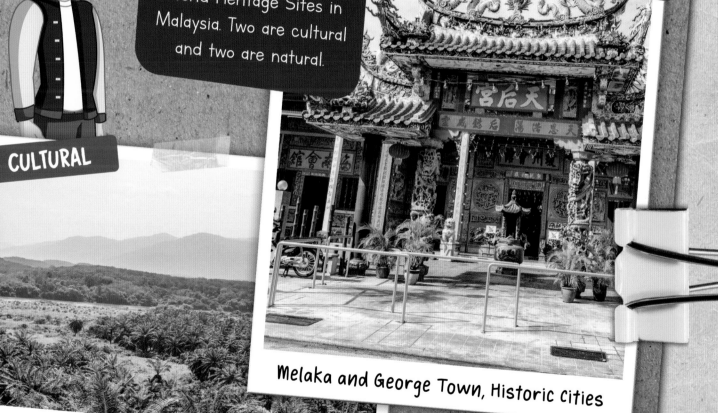

Melaka and George Town, Historic Cities

Archaeological Heritage of the Lenggong Valley

Don't Lose Your Head!

Tourists discover the culture of Borneo at the Mari Mari cultural village, which features five different tribes in one village. The most fearsome is the headhunting Murut tribe.

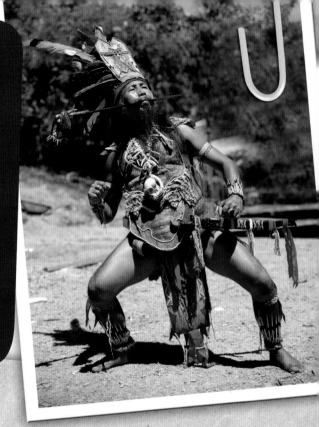

Malaysian Borneo

Off the mainland is East Malaysia and the states of Sarawak and Sabah on the island of Borneo. Malaysian Borneo is known for its beaches and diving spots, unique cultures and the natural diversity of its ancient rainforests and rich wildlife.

Borneo is believed to have the highest plant diversity of any region on earth. The world's largest flower, the Rafflesia, is found on Borneo. It is also home to thousands of bird and insect species, many of which aren't found anywhere else. Borneo's most famous residents are the orangutans and Sunda clouded leopards. While deforestation and hunting have depleted the numbers of these magnificent animals, there are successful conservation programs in place to help save them.

FLAG, SYMBOLS AND EMBLEMS

Flag of Malaysia

Malaysia's national flag consists of 14 red and white horizontal stripes, representing the 13 states and the Federal Government, with a dark blue rectangle in the upper left corner containing a yellow moon and star.

Coat of Arms

Adopted in 1965, Malaysia's Coat of Arms features two tigers supporting a shield (which serves as a representation of the Malaysian states). The crescent is the traditional symbol of Islam, while the star with 14 points represents the equal status of the 13 states of the federation and the Federal Government. The national motto, Bersekutu Bertambah Mutu which translates as 'Unity is Strength' is on the ribbon below.

National Flower

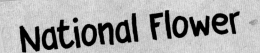

The Chinese Hibiscus is Malaysia's national flower.

National Anthem

Malaysia's national anthem is Negaraku meaning 'My Country'.

GLOSSARY

Bumiputras	Indigenous people of Malaysia
Colonialism	The control or governing influence of one nation over another country, territory or people
Dayaks	Indigenous people of Borneo
Kampong/Kampung	Malay village with traditional houses on stilts
Longhouse	Traditional dwelling for multiple Dayak families
Malacca/Melaka	A state and city in Malaysia
Palm oil	A type of edible vegetable oil and a major export for Malaysia
Ramadan	A month of fasting for Muslims
Sharia	Islamic law governing Muslims

Search key Words

Kuala Lumpur, Bahasa Melayu, Melaka, Malacca, Petronas Towers, Manglish, Borneo, palm oil

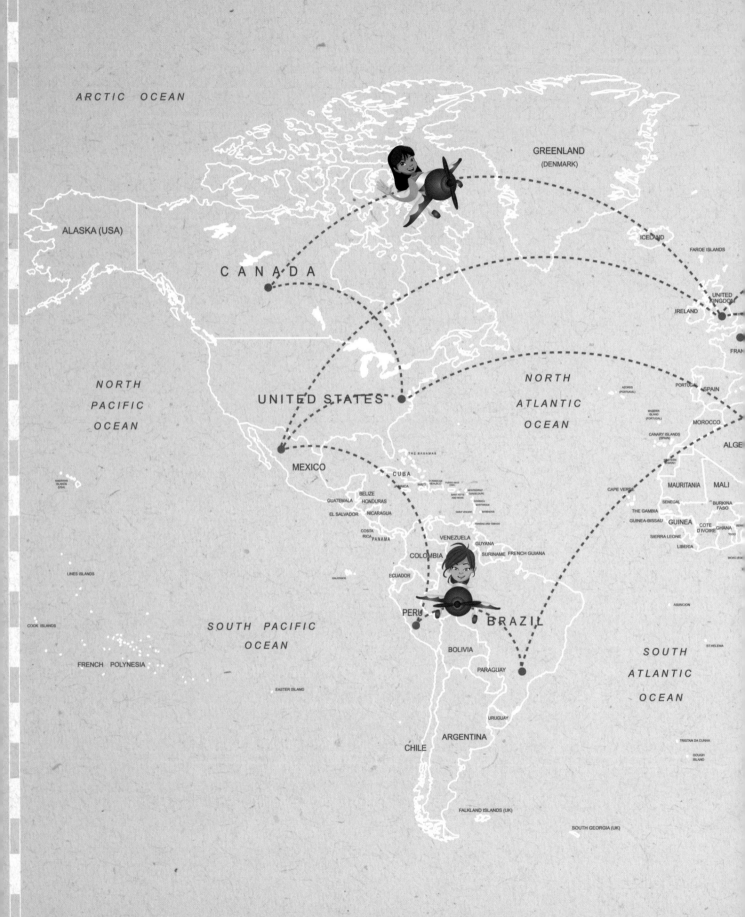